The WACKIEST WILDEST WEIRDEST

Animals in the World

Jack Hanna

Photography by
Rick A. Prebeg

THOMAS NELSON
Since 1798

NASHVILLE   DALLAS   MEXICO CITY   RIO DE JANEIRO   BEIJING

Published in Nashville, Tennessee, by Thomas Nelson. Thomas Nelson is a registered trademark of Thomas Nelson, Inc.

Cover and Interior Design: Birdsong Creative, Inc., Franklin, TN: www.birdsongcreative.com

Unless otherwise noted, photographs © 2009 by Rick A. Prebeg, World Class Images. Brown bears © 2009 by Columbus Zoo. Great white shark, octopus, and puffer fish photos © 2009 by Scott Johnson. Platypus photos reproduced with the kind permission of Healesville Sanctuary, Victoria, Australia. Large naked mole rat photo © 2009 by Skip Higgins. Small naked mole rat photo used with permission of National Geographic.

Thomas Nelson, Inc., titles may be purchased in bulk for educational, business, fund-raising, or sales promotional use. For information, please e-mail SpecialMarkets@ThomasNelson.com.

Library of Congress Cataloging-in-Publication Data

Hanna, Jack, 1947-
  Jungle Jack's wackiest, wildest, weirdest animals in the world / Jack Hanna ; photographs by Rick A. Prebeg.
    p. cm.
  ISBN 978-1-4003-1140-8 (hardcover)
  1. Exotic animals--Juvenile literature. 2. Animals--Juvenile literature. I. Prebeg, Rick A., ill. II. Title. III. Title: Wackiest, wildest, weirdest animals in the world.
  QL49.H2868 2009
  590--dc22

                                        2009000588
Printed in China
09 10 11 12 13 MT 6 5 4 3 2 1

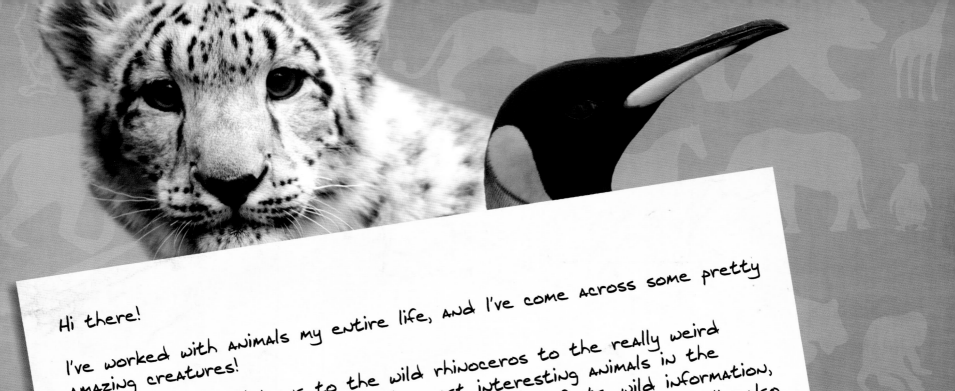

Hi there!

I've worked with animals my entire life, and I've come across some pretty amazing creatures!

From the wacky platypus to the wild rhinoceros to the really weird okapi, you are holding thirty of the most interesting animals in the world in your hands. You'll discover lots of wacky facts, wild information, and weird trivia, along with a few of my crazy animal adventures. I'm also including lots of photographs taken during my travels, so you'll see these guys up close and personal—just like I do!

In this wild life, I've tried to spread my amazement of and excitement about God's animal creations with everyone I meet. My hope is that your knowledge, love, and respect of these unique creatures will continue to grow as mine has. My own children—and now my grandchildren!—have shared some of these incredible encounters with me—and now I'd like to share them with you!

So join me now, as we meet some of the wackiest, wildest, weirdest animals in the world!

Your pal,

Jack Hanna

Jungle Jack Hanna

P.S. I've even included a DVD with footage from my adventures!

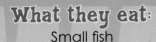

What they eat:
Small fish

Where they live:
Central and South American coasts and the Galápagos Islands

How big they get:
About 3 pounds, 30 to 34 inches long,
5-foot wingspan

BLUE-FOOTED BOOBY

What Makes Them Wacky

The name *blue-footed booby* alone would win a wacky contest, but this bird's name is just the beginning of its wackiness. Being a marine bird, it's naturally graceful in and over the water. Yet when those blue feet land on solid ground, this bird can be pretty clumsy.

That clumsiness doesn't stop the boys from trying to impress the girls with their zany dance moves. The male will hop from one foot to the other, holding one foot up high for the female to see. The boys know that, in the end, the one with the bluest feet wins! For the grand finale, the male whistles, the female honks, and they strut around together, pointing their beaks to the sky. What a crazy sight!

The blue-footed booby was probably named for the Spanish word *bobo*, which means "dunce" or "stupid."

The blue-footed booby is a *marine bird*. That means it spends most of its time in or around the ocean!

Baby blue-footed boobies eat fish that are regurgitated (swallowed and spit back up) from their parents' mouths. How'd you like *that* for dinner?!

BABOONS ARE BANANAS!

Watching a baboon troop is just like watching a wacky family interact. Once in Kenya, a huge group of a hundred or so baboons came by where we were staying. The big boss had a huge, furry mane and was leading the troop like a king. He was followed by mothers with babies hanging off or riding on their backs like little jockeys.

As they traveled, they would speak to one another through grunts, growls, barks, chirps, and even body language. They would shrug their shoulders, smack their lips, grin, and stare down their opponents. I've even heard they can fit six bananas in their mouth at one time. But don't try *that* one at home!

Can you guess the baboon's favorite pastime? He and his friends sit around for hours picking dead skin and insects from each other's fur. (Yeah, I think I'd stick with soccer!)

You can't miss the baboon's red backside! It's actually just calloused, nerveless skin that acts as a built-in seat cushion.

What Makes Them Wacky

Baboons have some really interesting habits. From their social structure to their daily schedules, they do a lot of things we do. In the mornings, the adults groom while the children play before they all head out as a group to hunt and feed with the dominant male as their guide. They take a break around lunchtime and then continue to forage the rest of the afternoon. At the end of the workday, they return to their homes where they clean up before retiring to bed. Sounds a lot like my daily schedule! What about yours?

BABOON

What they eat:
Bark, grasses, fruits, roots, birds, small mammals

Where they live:
The tall trees and savannas throughout Africa and Arabia

How big they get:
30 to 100 pounds, 20 to 50 inches tall

What they eat:
Mostly fish and squid

Where they live:
Icy plains of Antarctica

How big they get:
Up to 85 pounds, four feet tall

EMPEROR PENGUIN

What Makes Them Wacky

Just watching the wacky waddle of the emperor penguin can make you chuckle. Because they live in such harsh conditions, God designed penguins with some pretty heroic instincts that help their families survive and even thrive in the icy Antarctic climate.

The circle of life begins when the mom penguin leaves to look for food, while the dad penguin takes care of their egg. He protects the egg from the frigid earth by gently resting it on top of his feet and covering it with a fluffy layer of his tummy feathers called a *brood*. To survive the cold, the dads all huddle in a circle, protecting one another from the blustery snow. They share the warmth by rotating between the toasty interior and chilly exterior of the huddle.

In the meantime, the moms are out hunting for food to bring back to their newly hatched chicks. After two months, the moms return to take care of the chicks, while the hungry dads head to the ocean to feed.

The emperor penguin dives deep into the icy waters for food and can stay underwater for up to 20 minutes at a time!

The emperor is the largest of the penguins.

Emperor penguins can adapt to temperatures as low as −75°F. That's more than 100° below freezing! *Brrr!*

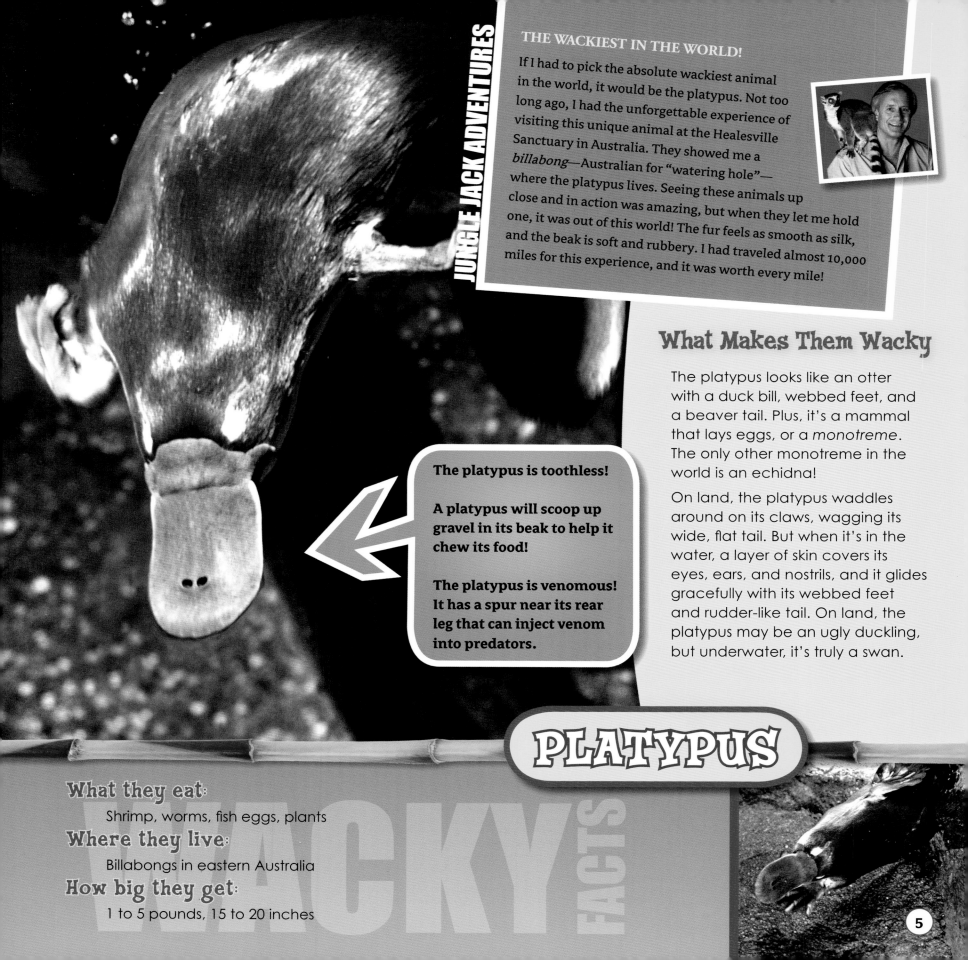

THE WACKIEST IN THE WORLD!

If I had to pick the absolute wackiest animal in the world, it would be the platypus. Not too long ago, I had the unforgettable experience of visiting this unique animal at the Healesville Sanctuary in Australia. They showed me a *billabong*—Australian for "watering hole"—where the platypus lives. Seeing these animals up close and in action was amazing, but when they let me hold one, it was out of this world! The fur feels as smooth as silk, and the beak is soft and rubbery. I had traveled almost 10,000 miles for this experience, and it was worth every mile!

What Makes Them Wacky

The platypus looks like an otter with a duck bill, webbed feet, and a beaver tail. Plus, it's a mammal that lays eggs, or a *monotreme*. The only other monotreme in the world is an echidna!

On land, the platypus waddles around on its claws, wagging its wide, flat tail. But when it's in the water, a layer of skin covers its eyes, ears, and nostrils, and it glides gracefully with its webbed feet and rudder-like tail. On land, the platypus may be an ugly duckling, but underwater, it's truly a swan.

The platypus is toothless!

A platypus will scoop up gravel in its beak to help it chew its food!

The platypus is venomous! It has a spur near its rear leg that can inject venom into predators.

PLATYPUS

WACKY FACTS

What they eat:
Shrimp, worms, fish eggs, plants

Where they live:
Billabongs in eastern Australia

How big they get:
1 to 5 pounds, 15 to 20 inches

What they eat:
Grasses, roots, fruits, vegetables

Where they live:
From the rocks to the swamps of Australia and New Zealand

How big they get:
10 to 40 pounds, 1½ to 6 feet from head to tail

WALLABY

What Makes Them Wacky

The wacky wallaby is very similar to—although smaller than—its cousin, the kangaroo. They're *macropods*, meaning they have big feet, and they're *marsupials*, meaning they have pouches where their young are raised.

When a *joey* (young wallaby) is born, it lives in its mom's pouch, eating and even peeing and pooping in there! (Most of it is absorbed into the pouch, but the mom still cleans it out on occasion.) A young wallaby will still hop back into its mom's pouch when it gets scared—even when it's so large that only its head will fit!

A full-grown female is called a *doe*, *flyer*, or *jill*, and a male is a *boomer*, *buck*, or *jack*—hey, I like that one!

There are some pretty weird types of wallabies: the pretty-faced, spectacled hare, toolache, red-necked, and swamp wallaby are just a few.

A wallaby can't hop backward.

The wallaby's tail acts like an extra leg, providing balance, steering, and more jumping power!

Baby wallabies weigh less than a paper clip when they're born!

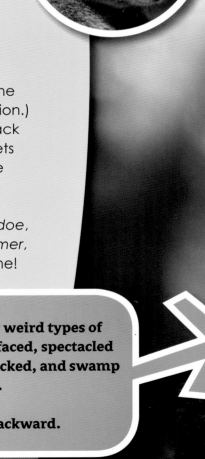

A young hyena is called a *whelp.*

Sometimes a group of hyenas will "bully" a cheetah away from its newly caught lunch!

Hyenas are more closely related to the cat than the dog.

What Makes Them Wacky

This scruffy, four-toed scavenger comes in striped, spotted, and solid brown varieties and sometimes has a wild mane to add to its ruffled appearance. Despite their uneven front and back legs, they can run up to 40 miles per hour! This helps these scavenging animals hunt their own dinner.

But whether their dinner is hunted or found, hyenas eat everything—the bones, hide, teeth—you name it. And whatever they can't digest, they spit back up in the form of pellets.

But the wackiest feature of the hyena has got to be the uncanny, human-like chuckle of the spotted hyena, used to express fear. Don't mistake it for a human laugh, though. In hyena, that chuckle says, "Run!"

HYENA

What they eat:
Animal carcasses or live prey if no carcasses are found

Where they live:
Plains, brush, and forests in Africa and India

How big they get:
90 to 190 pounds, 2½ to 7 feet long including tail

WACKY FACTS

What they eat:
Algae, insects, small fish, some shellfish

Where they live:
Near bodies of water in tropical and subtropical areas

How big they get:
5 to 8 pounds, 2½ to 5½ feet tall

FLAMINGO

What Makes Them Wacky

This beautiful pink bird is a *really* wacky eater! Perched on stilt-like legs, the flamingo will stick its head in the water upside down and shake its beak back and forth. The beak acts as a food filter, draining the water from the food particles.

And you know that bend in the middle of a flamingo's leg? It looks like a knee, but it's really an ankle! Its knee is close to the body, hidden by feathers.

Although it's a very wacky animal, watching a flamingo flock fly overhead is like watching a ballet in flight!

FLAMINGO GEOMETRY

Late one night after a show, I ended up stuck in a turnstile at an airport with a flamingo named Marty. Without thinking, I had pushed Marty's square crate into the pie-shaped area of the turnstile. Before I knew it, I was squished up against Marty's crate, and we were stuck. And with the turnstile stuck, I had also jammed the only exit from the airport with everyone trapped inside! Whoops.

To save the day, I wiggled like a worm to the top of the turnstile and went screaming for help. The nearby firemen were not amused—well, not until they saw that flamingo peeking through the bars of the turnstile. In the end, the firemen released Marty's crate, and I will never, *ever* again try to fit a square box into a round opening.

JUNGLE JACK ADVENTURES

Flamingos get their color from the pigments alpha- and beta-carotene—the important vitamins you eat in carrots!

Sometimes flamingos eat mud to help with their digestion!

What do a binturong and a movie theater have in common? They both smell like popcorn!

The binturong also comes complete with its very own chuckle, a sound it only makes when it's happy.

What Makes Them Wacky

Looking like an odd combination of a cat and a bear, the binturong is also known as the *bearcat*. While the nickname is much easier to say (and spell!), the binturong is neither bear nor cat, but it has similarities to both.

Like a bear, the binturong is an *omnivore* (it eats both plants and animals) and has coarse, thick fur. Its size, however, is more similar to a cat's, and the binturong also shares the feline's long whiskers and tail. Unlike the cat, however, a binturong's tail is *prehensile*, meaning it can grip like an extra hand. This comes in really handy as it climbs through the trees. God fully equipped this creature for a life in the forest, including back legs that can rotate around so that the claws will grip the trees while climbing down headfirst.

The binturong is the only animal known to digest the strangler fig tree seed. That makes it really important in replanting the rain forest, because it can replant the seeds with its droppings.

BINTURONG

What they eat:
Mostly fruits, but can eat eggs, rodents, or birds

Where they live:
Southeastern Asia

How big they get:
20 to 30 pounds, 20 to 40 inches long

WACKY FACTS

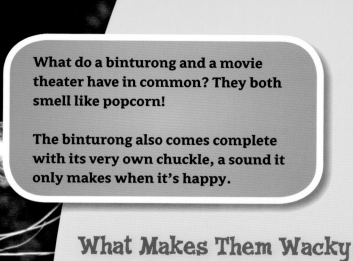

What they eat:
Ants, termites, worms, insect larvae

Where they live:
Scrublands in Australia and New Guinea

How big they get:
5 to 20 pounds, 1 to 2½ feet long

ECHIDNA

What Makes Them Wacky

This waddling, toothless, spiny creature is one of only two species of mammals that lay eggs. The mother lays a leathery, grape-sized egg, which hatches into a *puggle*. It stays in the mom's pouch until the puggle's spines start to develop—*yeowch!* The mom then places it in a burrow and comes back to feed it until it is ready to go out on its own.

The echidna has one big muscle that covers its whole body and helps it change shapes. When threatened, it rolls into a prickly ball, protecting its tender tummy. Other than the burrows for babies, echidnas don't really have one place to call home. They just wander the scrubby, brushy areas of Australia and New Guinea, sniffing around for their next log full of ants!

The echidna's ears are just little slits behind the eyes.

Check out its large, powerful claws, made especially for digging!

Echidnas have no teeth!

The echidna family name, *Tachyglossidae*, means "fast tongue." An echidna can stick out its tongue 100 times per minute! Can you?

What Makes Them Wacky

Under normal circumstances, the puffer swims along like any other fish. But threaten this little creature, and it turns the "wacky" volume up to high!

God created the puffer fish with the unique ability to inflate itself like a balloon when threatened. While the larger size and raised spikes may frighten away predators, the sudden increase in size makes it really difficult for the puffer to get anywhere fast. So, it just floats around, sometimes even upside down, until the threat is no longer visible. When all's clear, the puffer releases the air or water with a balloon-like sputter and goes back to its business.

The puffer has four teeth that are fused together to look like a small beak.

You can file the puffer fish in the "Don't Eat Me" category. They're highly toxic—even deadly—when eaten!

PUFFER FISH

they eat:

...hellfish, invertebrates, algae

...e they live:

...ear the coral bottoms of the Atlantic, Indian, and Pacific oceans; in ...rackish water (water that has a small amount of salt) and in freshwater

...big they get:

...to 24 inches long

What they eat:
Leaves, twigs, branches, bushes

Where they live:
Grasslands, savannas, and shrublands of eastern, central, and southern Africa

How big they get:
About 1 to 1½ tons,
5 feet tall at the shoulder

BLACK RHINOCEROS

What Makes Them Wild

This critically endangered mammal is a treasure in the wild. Some people value the black rhino for its enormous size, its tank-like prehistoric appearance, and its mere survival as a species. Sadly, poachers also value the black rhino, but only for the money its horn will bring. Poachers sell the horn for so-called "medicinal" purposes and for making knife handles and other carved items. As a result, the black rhino population was reduced by 90 percent in the late twentieth century.

The good news is that this tough-as-nails creature is making a comeback! Slowly but surely—thanks to well-guarded rhino sanctuaries—the number of black rhinos in the wild continues to grow, giving us all the more reason to celebrate this amazing giant of God's creation.

The black rhino is a walking feeding ground for birds, such as oxpeckers and egrets. They eat the parasites living on the rhino's skin. Yum!

What do rhinos use for sunscreen and insect repellent? Mud! That may get you some strange looks at the beach!

Rhino horns are made of *keratin*—material that is also in your fingernails and hair. Unlike most horns (and like our hair), the rhino horn is connected at the skin, not the skull.

The black rhino has a *prehensile* upper lip. That means its lip can reach out, grasp food, and pull it into the rhino's mouth! Try that one at dinner tonight!

A FAVORITE FRIEND

I've been around elephants since I was a teenager, and they have never ceased to amaze me. Back then it was helping a veterinarian with a feisty African bull elephant at the Knoxville Zoo. And today it's coming face-to-face with a baby at an elephant orphanage in Kenya.

The most fascinating thing I've learned about this animal is what we *haven't* learned about them, such as the extent of their intelligence and social behaviors. Elephants have been known to feel vibrations in their feet, walking toward thunderstorms 100 miles away in search of water. Older females can remember friendly faces. One of my favorite elephants here at the zoo used to untie my shoelaces! The more I learn about these amazing animals, the more I want to know.

In an elephant's trunk alone, there are about 40,000 muscles! You have only 600 to 800 muscles in your entire body.

An elephant drinks up to 50 gallons of water per day. How about you?

What Makes Them Wild

The African elephant is the largest land mammal in the world. But there is so much more to this gentle giant than its size. For one thing, the elephant's trunk is a wildly versatile tool. It can be used as a snorkel, a smeller, a vacuum, a blower, a grabber, a trumpet, an ear scratcher, a baby snuggler, and so much more.

Though they seem very gentle, you surely don't want to be in the path of a charging elephant. The lion may be considered the king of the jungle, but the elephant is one animal that even the lion knows better than to mess with.

AFRICAN ELEPHANT

What they eat:
Leaves, grasses, fruits, bark

Where they live:
African woodlands and savannas south of the Sahara Desert

How big they get:
7 tons, up to 13 feet tall at the shoulder

WILD FACTS

What they eat:

Marine mammals, fish, even sea turtles and birds

Where they live:

Medium-temperature coastal waters around the world

How big they get:

Up to 1 ton, 13 to 21 feet long

GREAT WHITE SHARK

What Makes Them Wild

The great white shark was designed to be a lean, mean hunting machine. This ocean-bound fish glides stealthily through the water, camouflaged by a pattern called *countershading*. The great white's top half is gray, and the bottom half is white. When looked down on from above, it seems to be part of the ocean floor. And when viewed from below, the white blends nicely with the sunny waters above.

Having powerful jaws armed with rows of super sharp, serrated (saw-like) teeth that reload when broken, this shark eats pretty much whatever it wants. Human shark bites are many times believed to be a result of curiosity, as the shark uses its teeth to identify floating objects. But the great white prefers the calorie-loaded fat of sea lions and seals for the most efficient fuel.

A shark's skin looks rubbery, but it actually feels like sandpaper.

A great white shark can survive for three months without food!

Each shark can lose up to 30,000 teeth in a lifetime! We only lose only about 20 teeth in our lifetime.

Great white sharks are *ovoviviparous*: that is a big, funny word that means the baby's egg hatches inside the mother.

CHARGE!

Once when I was on safari in East Africa, I got a little *too* up close and personal with a Cape buffalo. I was just walking back from dinner, minding my own business. Then I heard a rustle, followed by a thunder, as I looked up to see a Cape buffalo coming at me from out of nowhere. He was charging toward me full force, and all I could see were those U-shaped horns headed my way! In that split second, I jumped behind a tree, and those horns missed me by only inches. The buffalo kept on going, but I think I stayed behind that tree for 30 minutes before coming out to see if the coast were clear.

What Makes Them Wild

At first glance, this cow-like mammal seems to be pretty harmless. However, the Cape buffalo (also known as the *African buffalo*) is considered one of the most aggressive animals in Africa, right up there with lions, hippos, and rhinos. Their horns can be deadly weapons.

A popular target for hunters, the Cape buffalo returns the favor by seeking out hunters who have harmed it in the past. Because humans are the Cape buffalo's main predator, it has become quite suspicious of this two-legged stranger and will not hesitate to charge when it feels threatened.

The skin of a Cape buffalo is very thick—even as much as two inches thick around the neck!

The Cape buffalo will never go farther than a day's walk from a water source.

CAPE BUFFALO

WILD FACTS

What they eat:
Mostly grasses, but also shrubs and other plants

Where they live:
Savannas and forests in eastern, central, and southern Africa

How big they get:
Up to 1,000 pounds, 5½ feet tall at the shoulder

What they eat:
Fish, small mammals, plants, roots; have been known to take down moose and caribou

Where they live:
Near streams in Canada, Asia, Europe, and the northwestern United States (mainly Alaska)

How big they get:
Up to 1,400 pounds, 9 feet tall

BROWN BEAR

What Makes Them Wild

The brown bear tops my list of the wildest animals in North America. When standing on its hind legs, this mammal towers over the average adult. Throw in a set of claws as long as human fingers, and you've got one mighty creature that you certainly don't want to mess with. Like most wild animals, the brown bear doesn't go after humans unless it feels threatened, especially if it feels there's a threat to its young.

One of the most interesting habits of the brown bear is *hibernation*. As winter approaches, the bear will binge on food to build up a large supply of fat before digging a den for a winter-long nap. It won't wake up to eat or drink, and mother bears don't even wake up when their cubs are born. The hairless babies, weighing less than a pound, just snuggle up and nurse until spring arrives.

Alaska is home to 98 percent of the population of brown bears in the United States.

When a brown bear stands up on its hind legs, it's usually not to threaten but just to better see and smell its surroundings. Still, that doesn't mean you need to stick around and find out!

Because their colors vary greatly, it's hard to identify brown bears by color alone. Unlike the black bear, the brown bear has a hump between its shoulders and long, straight claws.

A male lion marks his territory the same way a male dog does. . . .

A lion's roar can be heard up to five miles away! That's the loudest roar of all the big cats!

A lion can eat more than 60 pounds of food in one meal. For you and me, that would be 240 quarter-pound hamburgers!

What Makes Them Wild

The infamous lion is probably the best known of all the wild animals. You'll find this majestically maned mammal on everything from currency to family crests, statues to storybooks, as a symbol of great power.

It's very true that lions are keen hunters. But these animals are much more than mindless predators. They have a highly developed social structure, traveling in families, or *prides*, made up of males, females, and cubs. And when resting, they display affection by licking and rubbing necks. It's no wonder that this giant cat is considered to be the king of the beasts!

LION

WILD FACTS

What they eat:
Medium to large mammals

Where they live:
Savannas and grasslands in sub-Saharan Africa, with a very few in northwestern India

How big they get:
Up to 700 pounds, 4 feet tall at the shoulder

What they eat:
Medium-sized animals, sometimes even birds and fish

Where they live:
From mountains to deserts in sub-Saharan Africa and parts of Asia

How big they get:
200 pounds, up to 9½ feet long including tail

LEOPARD

What Makes Them Wild

There are several types of leopards—spotted, snow, clouded—living in a wide variety of habitats and conditions. Unlike their lion cousins, leopards are generally solitary animals. They live alone in the wild, except when raising their cubs.

Their beautiful coat serves a much more practical purpose; it camouflages the leopard from predator and prey, breaking up the outline of its body with a multicolored pattern. The color of a leopard's coat depends on its typical environment. Leopards found in grasslands have lighter coats than those in dense forests to help them better blend in with their surroundings. During the night, this sleek mammal goes virtually unseen, stalking and pouncing on its prey.

To protect its catch from scavenging lions and hyenas, the leopard will many times use its superior climbing ability to carry its dinner high into the trees, where the other scavengers are unable to reach it. After its nightly feast, the leopard will stretch out on a comfy limb and relax, escaping the heat of the day.

The snow leopard is an amazing jumper. It can leap 50 feet forward and 20 feet high!

When you hear a sawing noise on your next safari, scan the grasses and trees. You may actually be hearing a leopard call!

If you look closely, you'll see that the leopard isn't clearly "spotted" like the cheetah. The leopard's pattern is made up of circular groups of spots called *rosettes*.

The Tasmanian devil is the largest meat-eating marsupial in the world!

Unlike most marsupials, the Tassie's pouch opens to the rear, which makes it pretty difficult for a mom to peek in on her babies.

What Makes Them Wild

With its coarse, bear-like fur, the shape of a rat, and the size of a small dog, this Tasmanian marsupial won't win any beauty contests. When you add its ear-shattering screech and an . . . er, um . . . foul odor emitted when stressed, this poor guy isn't likely to win any popularity contests either. But pound for pound, it's one of the toughest animals out there. This aggressive little creature can take down animals much larger than itself, but it prefers to take the easier route for dinner: *carrion*, also known as roadkill and carcasses. When it sniffs out a meal, it lets nothing go to waste, devouring the animal— bones, skin, and all!

If you've seen a Tasmanian devil at a zoo, consider yourself lucky. They were once found only in Australian zoos, but conservationists are working to raise awareness by getting Tasmanian devils to a zoo near you!

TASMANIAN DEVIL

What they eat:
Small mammals, birds, sometimes even reptiles and frogs

Where they live:
Logs, caves, and burrows in Tasmania, Australia

How big they get:
8 to 26 pounds, 20 to 30 inches long

What they eat:
Mammals, fish, amphibians, reptiles

Where they live:
In and around the waters of tropical South America

How big they get:
Up to 500 pounds, 20 to 30 feet long

ANACONDA

What Makes Them Wild

An anaconda—sometimes called a *water boa*—is an enormous, nonvenomous reptile in the boa constrictor family. The anaconda strikes out and bites its dinner, using its 100-plus backward-curved teeth to hold the prey in place as the rest of its body coils around the animal. It kills its prey by *constricting*, or squeezing, it until the animal can no longer breathe. When the animal is lifeless, the snake begins to slide the food through its mouth into its stomach. The anaconda doesn't chew its food, but allows the strong acid in its stomach to digest the animal—bones and all!

FINGER FOOD

While filming an anaconda segment, I noticed that our star had a loose piece of skin dangling from its nose. When I reached up to pick it off, much too carelessly, it snatched up my finger and clamped down on it like a vise with a hundred or more teeth.

"Don't move!" Stan, the herpetologist, instructed.

It wasn't like I could anyway. So I just waited patiently—well, as patiently as a person can wait with his finger in an anaconda's mouth. Finally, they found an old shoe and pried the snake's mouth open. I carefully, but quickly, pulled my finger free. It was completely shredded—still intact—but with about two dozen punctures. Now, I'm all about viewing wildlife up close, but next time I'll keep my hands to myself.

JUNGLE JACK ADVENTURES

The anaconda is the largest type of snake in the world! At birth, it is already one to two feet long!

Like other snakes, the anaconda smells with its tongue. It also has glands that create a foul-smelling musk, which is poisonous to insects.

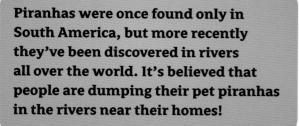

Piranhas were once found only in South America, but more recently they've been discovered in rivers all over the world. It's believed that people are dumping their pet piranhas in the rivers near their homes!

Piranhas are said to be a tasty treat—if you can catch them. Their teeth tend to cut the fishing line. And if that doesn't happen, other piranhas are likely to try to eat the distressed fish before it gets out of the water!

The word *piranha* is believed to come from two words in the Tupi Indian language meaning "fish" and "tooth."

What Makes Them Wild

All legends aside, the piranha does have quarter-inch, razor-sharp teeth, but it prefers to scavenge for food. If there's a food shortage, piranhas do become more aggressive.

The most extreme stories—of blood-boiling, piranha-filled water that leaves only bones behind—aren't typical. A school of piranhas, when hungry, can clean the carcass of an animal quickly and methodically by taking a bite, then moving over for the next fish to take a bite. This constant movement creates a "boiling" appearance on the surface. But this occurrence is also rare. While you may not lose your life to one of these wild-looking fish, you probably don't want to stick your finger in its mouth either.

PIRANHA

WILD FACTS

What they eat:
Fish, small birds, reptiles

Where they live:
Rivers of eastern and central South America

How big they get:
8 to 20 inches long

What they eat:
Leaves, flowers, twigs

Where they live:
Dense forests in western and central Africa

How big they get:
Up to 900 pounds, 3 to 4½ feet tall

BONGO

What Makes Them Weird

With its long, vertical white stripes, the bongo looks like the zebra's long-lost cousin. Unlike the zebra, however, this mammal is a type of antelope, and a unique one at that! For one, it's the largest, heaviest forest antelope. It's also the only tragelaphid species in which both the male and female have the spiral horns that give these creatures their mythical appearance.

Looking quite majestic while running, the bongo leans its head way back, turning up its nose. This running style makes it more aerodynamic and keeps it from becoming tangled in the thick forest branches.

Bongos are shy, solitary animals. Partly because of a long history of bongo hunting, they are quite skittish—and *nocturnal* (more active at night)—making it very difficult to see them in the wild or to get a realistic count of how many there really are in existence.

The rusty color of a bongo's fur will rub right off on your hands!

The bongo is a type of *tragelaphid*, a spiral-horned antelope.

Here is a photo of Don Hunt and me with a bongo. Don has dedicated his life to bongo preservation through the Mount Kenya Wildlife Conservancy.

THE TERMITE BUFFET

Once, while in Brazil, I saw the most spectacular sight—anteaters in the wild! I just sat and watched them as they shuffled around on their knuckles (actually their under-turned claws), wandering through a buffet of termite mounds. These mounds were as hard as rocks and solid as concrete, but the anteaters could just tear into them with their sharp, powerful claws and . . . lunchtime! As they meandered along, sniffing around for the best meal—and sometimes even standing up on their back legs to get a better view—they would fan out their huge, bushy tails like an umbrella to protect themselves from the sun. They are truly one of the weirdest animals I've ever seen!

What Makes Them Weird

When you come nose-to-oddly-long-nose with this mammal, you know you're looking at one of the weirdest animals in the world. That long nose provides a powerful sense of smell, which makes up for this animal's really bad eyesight. Protruding ears frame the anteater's long, skinny face and blue, whipping tongue—built for searching in the small holes where insects live. Add to that a coarse-haired body and a super long, bushy tail, and you've got hard evidence that God has a great sense of humor!

> **The giant anteater consumes more than 30,000 insects each day!**
>
> **This animal's tongue is more than 2 feet long! Have you measured your tongue lately?**

GIANT ANTEATER

What they eat:
Small insects, mostly ants and termites

Where they live:
Forests, grasslands, and swamps of Central and South America

How big they get:
Up to 90 pounds, 7 feet long including tail

WEIRD FACTS

What they eat:
Mostly insects and grubs, but sometimes fruits

Where they live:
Burrows in warm grasslands, semideserts, rain forests, and marshes in North, Central, and South America

How big they get:
Depending on the species, 3 ounces to 120 pounds, 5 inches to 5 feet long

ARMADILLO

What Makes Them Weird

The smallest species of armadillo (the pink fairy) is as small as your hand, while the largest (the giant armadillo) is almost as big as a high schooler! And there's a different color of armadillo for every day of the week (well, almost): pink, red, yellow, gray, brown, and black! The three-banded armadillo is probably the most remarkable, with its ability to roll its entire body into a little ball. It tucks its nose into its tummy to create a hard, shell-like sphere that is almost impenetrable to predators!

Armadillo means "little armored one." Check out this guy's built-in armored plates!

The plate on each armadillo's head is unique—just like human fingerprints.

THE AMAZING THREE-BANDED B.J. AND BONITA!

Two of the Columbus Zoo's three-banded armadillos star in most of my live shows. B.J. and Bonita are such meek and interesting creatures—they're perfect for some after-show mingling too. "Awws" erupt when one of them pokes its little nose out to say hi to (and sniff out) the crowd. Everyone is eager to feel the bone-like plates that protect their bodies. It's at that moment when we offer this tidbit: "Oh, and did you know that armadillos are one of the only animals known to carry leprosy?" That usually gets their attention! Of course, like 95 percent of armadillos, ours do not carry the dreaded skin disease.

Another less startling—but equally amazing—tidbit is that armadillos are able to hear worms underground. I'm still not sure how anyone knows this. I once found a worm on my driveway and tried to listen to it. I didn't hear a thing.

JUNGLE JACK ADVENTURES

Both the "two-toed" and "three-toed" sloths have three claws on their hind feet. You'll need to count their front claws to identify them correctly.

The sloth poops only about once a week. Enough said.

Sloths get some of their nutrients from licking the bacteria growing on their fur. . . . I think I'll just take my vitamins!

What Makes Them Weird

Even if the sloth doesn't win the World's Weirdest Animal award, it has got to be the world's slowest! This sluggish, tree-dwelling mammal has coarse, shaggy fur, which often has algae growing on it and beetles and moths living in it!

Despite its slow pace, the sloth is a skilled climber, moving from tree to tree through the high branches in the treetops. When the sloth does inch its way to the ground to use the bathroom, it resorts to an awkward army crawl. Perhaps the quickest a sloth moves is—oddly enough—when it occasionally drops from the rain forest trees to take a swim in the waters below. In spite of its many oddities, one look at the ever-smiling face of this docile creature is certain to be love at first sight.

SLOTH

What they eat:
Tree leaves, but the two-toed sloth will sometimes eat insects and lizards

Where they live:
High in the trees of Central and South America

How big they get:
Up to 17 pounds, 30 inches long

WEIRDEST FACTS

What they eat:
Grasses, flowers, seeds, plants, and sometimes small creatures, such as insects and lizards

Where they live:
Savannas and brushlands throughout sub-Saharan Africa

How big they get:
Up to 350 pounds, 9 feet tall

OSTRICH

What Makes Them Weird

This odd bird is at the top of its class in several subjects! The ostrich is both the tallest and the heaviest of all birds. It's also the fastest two-legged animal! Even when *all*-legged animals are considered, the ostrich still comes in second only to the cheetah.

This flightless bird also packs a powerful kick! Plus, with a four-inch claw on each foot, it can even kill a lion! But kicking is usually the last resort. First, to escape being seen, the ostrich will squat low to the ground with its neck laid out flat in front of it. If the bird still feels threatened, it will kick those long legs into high gear. Using its wings for steering and balance, it will likely outrun whatever is chasing it.

BALLERINA BIRD!

The ostrich is without a doubt the weirdest bird in the world! Just looking at it, I wonder, *What was God thinking when He built that thing?* It's like a nine-foot ballerina with a big black tutu—and a ballerina's kick to match! Unfortunately, I was once on the receiving end of such a kick, and I'll tell you, that's one ballerina bird you don't want to mess with!

The Kalahari bushmen in Africa are accustomed to these large birds, even using their six-inch eggs as canteens. On one trip, I was taught how to ride an ostrich! But I wouldn't suggest trying that in the wild. For starters, you'd never be able to catch one!

JUNGLE JACK ADVENTURES

An ostrich can run up to 45 miles per hour! That makes it the fastest animal on two legs!

The ostrich has only two toes on each foot—but I wouldn't get close enough to count them!

Most groups of birds are called *flocks*, but groups of ostriches are called *herds*.

To tell the male from a female, look for horns—the little nubs on each side of the head. Males have them; females don't.

What Makes Them Weird

There are bugs . . . and then there are Madagascar hissing cockroaches! Its most notably weird quality is the hissing noise it makes when disturbed, fighting, or mating. Other insects make noise through vibrations or rubbing their legs together, but this unique hiss is created when the bug blows air through its breathing holes. It's a sound you'll never forget!

Another odd quality is its lack of wings, which most cockroaches do have. But the hisser does just fine without them. It is an exceptional climber, even able to scurry up surfaces as slick as glass. Unlike its cousin, which has earned the cockroach a bad name, the Madagascar hissing cockroach isn't a pest and prefers the dark forest floor over human habitats any day.

Some hissing cockroaches grow to be longer than your index finger!

Instead of laying eggs in a nest, the mom hissing cockroach has a built-in nest, a little egg case inside her body where she stores her babies until they hatch.

HISSING COCKROACH

What they eat:
Fruits or plants that litter the forest floor

Where they live:
Forest floors on the island of Madagascar

How big they get:
About 1 ounce, 2 to 3 inches long

WEIRD FACTS

What they eat:

Small sea creatures from plankton to crabs (depending on size of species)

Where they live:

Ocean waters all over the world

How big they get:

110 pounds, up to a 16-foot armspan

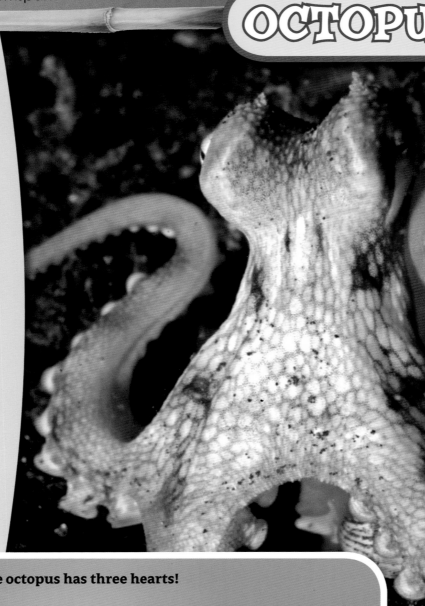

OCTOPUS

What Makes Them Weird

There is no way to pick a favorite from the 300-plus types of octopus! From their suction-cup-covered arms to their bird-like beaks, these boneless, shell-less wads of *mantle* (the muscle that covers their bodies) all share features that make them some of the weirdest creatures ever.

As a means of defense, the octopus can change its color quickly to match the color and even the texture of its surroundings. If that doesn't work, it shoots a cloud of black ink into the water to confuse its predators. And as a last resort, it can even dismember itself, leaving a lone, twitching arm as a distraction or simply to break free. The octopus will grow a new arm to replace it! A less noticeable feature is its beak—containing venomous saliva—which can take a chunk out of predators and prey alike!

The octopus has three hearts!

Some types of octopuses can lay more than 200,000 eggs at a time! (But only a couple will survive to be adults.)

Each arm of the giant Pacific octopus can grow to more than six feet long!

The okapi doesn't need cotton swabs; it can lick its own ears!

During the first two months of its life, the baby okapi hides in the growth of the forest floor. During this time, it doesn't even poop!

An adult okapi can eat up to 65 pounds of food a day!

What Makes Them Weird

A close relative of the giraffe, the okapi appears to be an odd mixture of giraffe, horse, and zebra. With its slender head and big ears similar to the giraffe's, the okapi also has a *prehensile* tongue in common, which it uses to grab leaves from trees. The okapi is about the size of a horse, with a velvety brown middle. But its legs are all zebra! Strange as it appears, this pattern helps the okapi blend in with the sun-streaked forest.

And it must be doing a great job! The okapi was not discovered by Western scientists until 1908. More recently, it was feared extinct because it hadn't been seen in the wild since 1958. But in 2008, some 50 years later, it was finally photographed in the wild—for the first time ever—proving its survival!

OKAPI

What they eat:
Leaves, grasses, fruits, fungi, and even charcoal

Where they live:
Forests of the Democratic Republic of the Congo in Africa

How big they get:
About 550 pounds, 7 feet long, 5½ feet tall at the shoulder

What they eat:
Insects, but sometimes lizards and small birds

Where they live:
Trees and bushes of Africa, Madagascar, Europe, and Asia

How big they get:
Up to 2 pounds, more than 2 feet long

CHAMELEON

What Makes Them Weird

Just when you think things can't get any weirder, here comes the chameleon! This reptile comes in large and small, horned and unhorned varieties. But its most amazing trait is its ability to change colors to blend into its surroundings. The trick is in the *chromatophores*, or cells containing different colored pigments that make up multiple layers of skin. The change in color can be in response to stress, temperature, humidity, lighting, mood, or even just to attract a mate.

The chameleon's cone-shaped eyes move it up several notches on the weird scale too, with its ability to move each eye in a different direction—at the same time! This allows the chameleon to see all around it and even focus on two objects at once. And to seal the weird deal, just add in its long, sticky tongue that shoots out at lightning speed, forms a suction cup on the end, and snatches insects up to a body length away. That's weird enough for me!

How do you tell a male from a female chameleon? Just check the number of toes on the back foot. A male has three; a female four.

Chameleon means "earth lion."

A chameleon's tongue is sometimes longer than its body!

The naked mole rat isn't a mole . . . or a rat. Its closest relatives are porcupines, chinchillas, and guinea pigs.

Naked mole rats can run as fast backward as they can forward!

Naked mole rats can live 30 years or more!

The naked mole rat uses its teeth for digging! Its mouth is specially designed to close behind the teeth to keep it from getting a mouthful of dirt while working.

What Makes Them Weird

Like a hairless, wrinkly mouse with beaver teeth, this little mammal is so ugly, it's adorable.

Under the baked earthen floors of Africa, these guys are hard at work, active in an amazing social structure. Naked mole rats are *eusocial*, meaning each individual is set to perform a certain function—breeder, soldier, worker—for its entire life. Some insects, like bees and ants, are eusocial too, but naked mole rats are the only mammals with a structure this complex.

Naked mole rats spend almost their entire lives underground, building maze-like tunnels. The diggers line up, acting like a conveyer belt and tossing the dirt behind them.

Amazing animals? Yes. But just one look, and you know we've gone beyond the realm of weird.

NAKED MOLE RAT

WEIRD FACTS

What they eat:
Roots and tubers (such as potatoes or yams)

Where they live:
Tunnels under very dry regions and savannas of East Africa

How big they get:
2½ ounces, up to 7 inches including tail

Animal Sanctuary: n. a place where animals are brought to be protected.

Billabong: n. a small lake or pond, particularly in Australia.

Bird: n. warm-blooded, egg-laying vertebrate; set apart by feathers, wings, and a beak.

Brackish: adj. a mixture of both salt water and freshwater.

Endangered: adj. to be at risk of extinction.

Extinct: adj. no longer alive, mainly in reference to an entire species.

Fish: n. cold-blooded water vertebrate, usually having scales and breathing through gills.

Flock: n. a group of birds.

Habitat: n. the dwelling place where an animal naturally lives.

Herd: n. a group of animals, typically large mammals such as elephants, buffalo, and cattle, but also used to reference groups of ostriches, which are birds.

Herpetologist: n. a zoologist who studies reptiles and amphibians.

Hibernation: n. the resting state in which some animals spend winter.

Insect: n. small, arthropod invertebrate that is more or less obviously segmented with a well-defined head, thorax, and abdomen.

Invertebrate: n. an animal that does not have a backbone or spinal column.

Keratin: n. a tough substance in hair, nails, horns, and hooves.

Macropod: a type of marsupial, literally meaning "big feet."

Mammal: n. warm-blooded vertebrate typically noted by hair on skin, and with the exception of monotremes, gives birth to live young.

Mantle: n. a protective layer of skin in mollusks or brachiopods.

Marine: adj. of or relating to the sea.

Marsupial: n. a mammal that births underdeveloped young and cares for them inside a pouch.

Monotreme: n. a type of mammal that does not bear live young, but instead lays eggs.

Nocturnal: adj. to be active during the night.

Ovoviviparous: adj. hatching living eggs inside the body.

Poacher: n. someone who fishes or hunts illegally.

Predator: n. an animal that lives by hunting and eating other animals.

Prehensile: adj. adapted for holding, grasping, or wrapping around an object.

Prey: n. an animal hunted or caught for food.

Regurgitate: v. to spit up food that has been swallowed.

Reptile: n. cold-blooded, egg-laying vertebrate.

Savanna: n. flat grassland in tropical or subtropical regions.

Scavenger: n. an animal that feeds on dead animals or other discarded food.

School: n. a group of fish.

Tachyglossidae: n. echidna, from the Latin meaning "fast tongue."

Tragelaphid: n. spiral-horned antelope.

Troop: n. a group of animals, specifically monkeys, kangaroos, or bees.

Venomous: adj. having a gland or glands that secrete venom, a poison, and being able to inflict a poisonous wound by biting or stinging.

Vertebrate: n. an animal that has a backbone or spinal column.